AMERICAN MUSCLE CARS

COLORING BOOK

FOR KIDS

KATE TAYLOR DESIGN

The book contains 40 freehand illustrations. A second section of the book includes the same car images printed in a smaller size to test colors and techniques.

If you would like to reorder, please scan the QR Code

1970 CHEVROLET CHEVELLE

1970 DODGE CHARGER RT

1969 SHELBY MUSTANG GT350

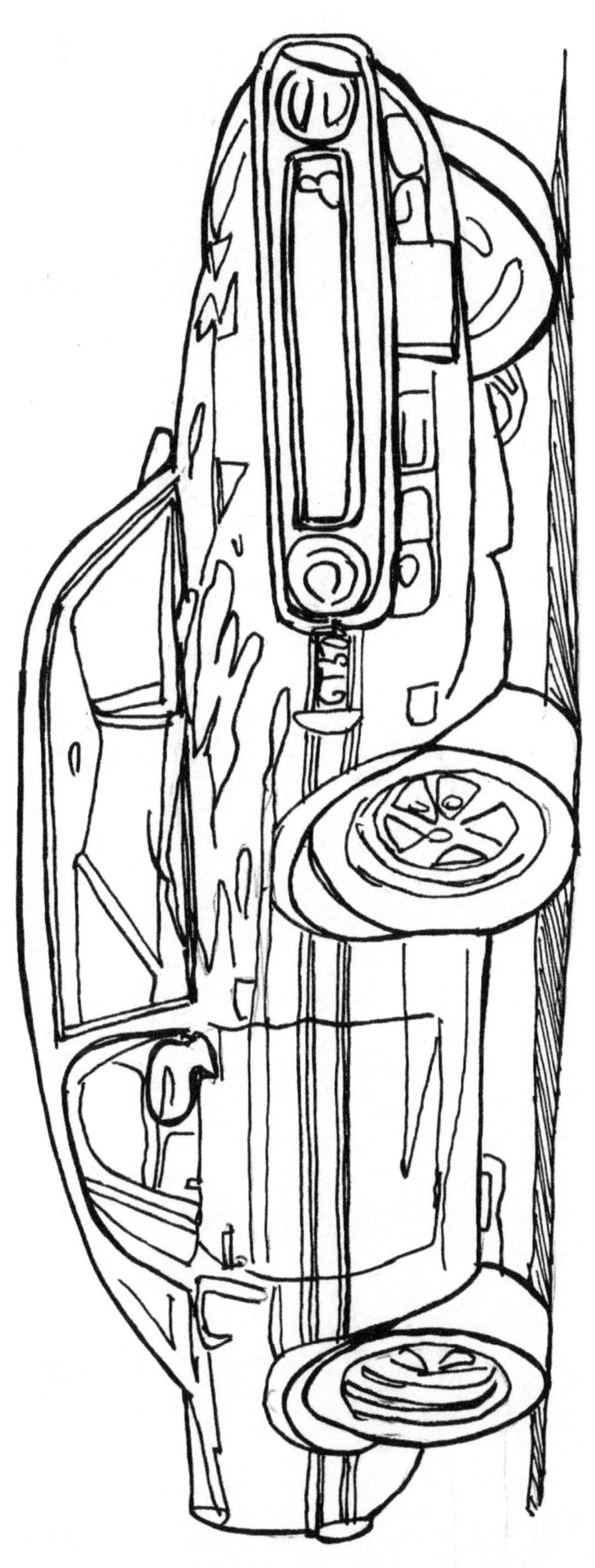

1969 SHELBY GT500 FASTBACK

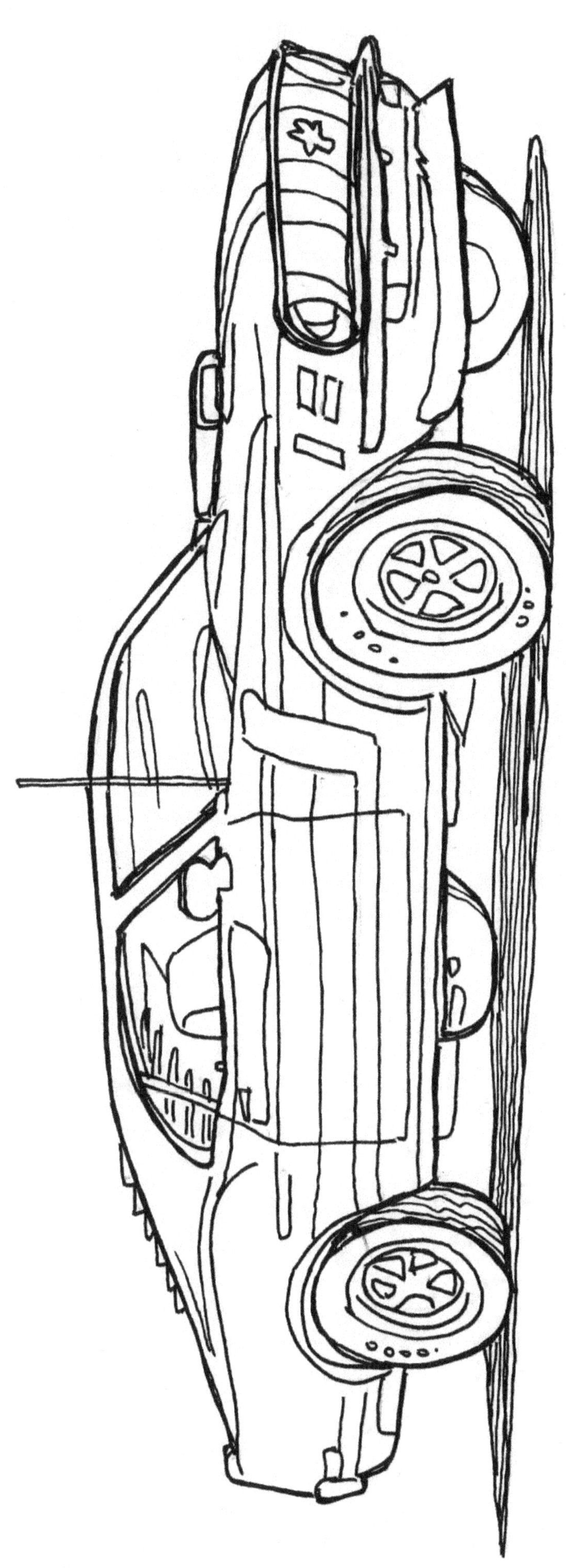

1970 FORD MUSTANG BOSS 302

1970 CORONET R/T

1969 FORD MUSTANG BOSS

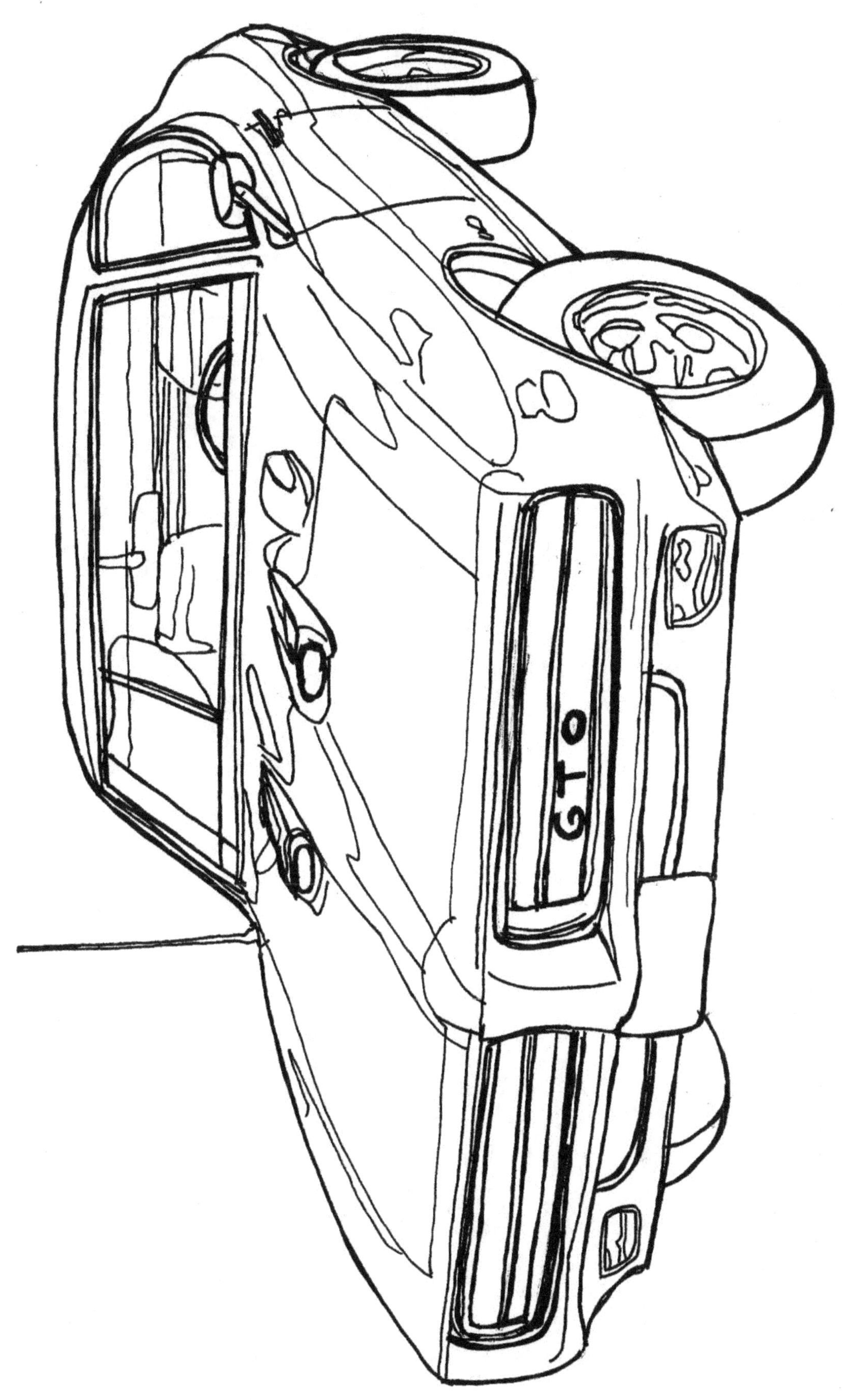

GTO
1969 PONTIAC GTO

1970 CORONET SUPER BEE

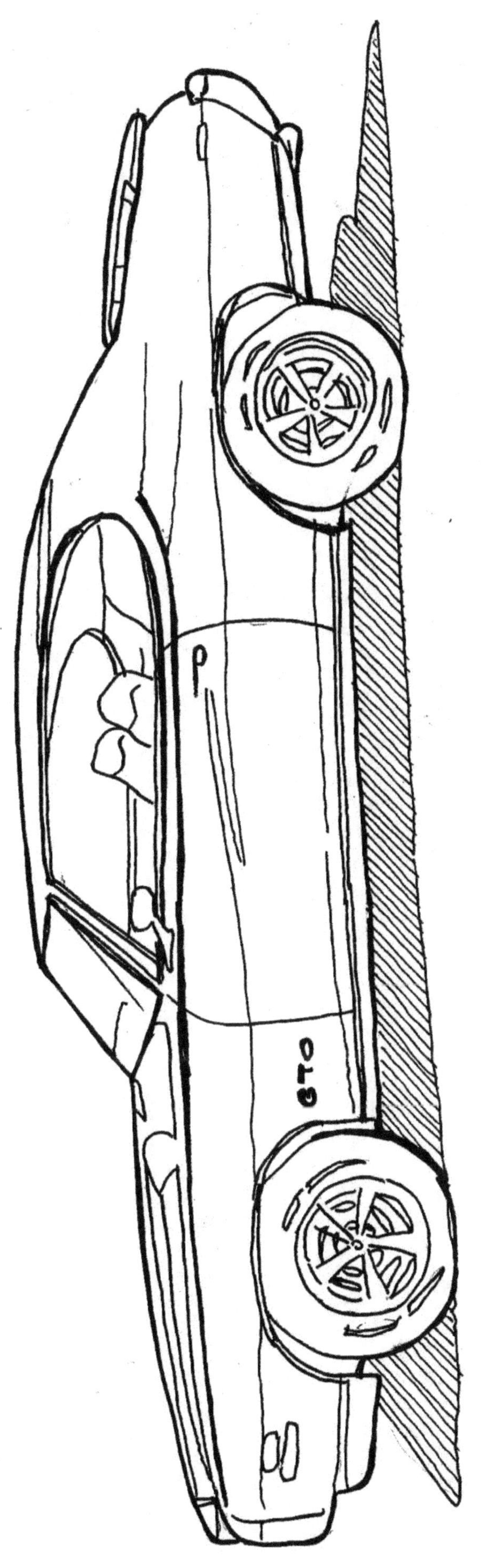

1969 PONTIAC GTO

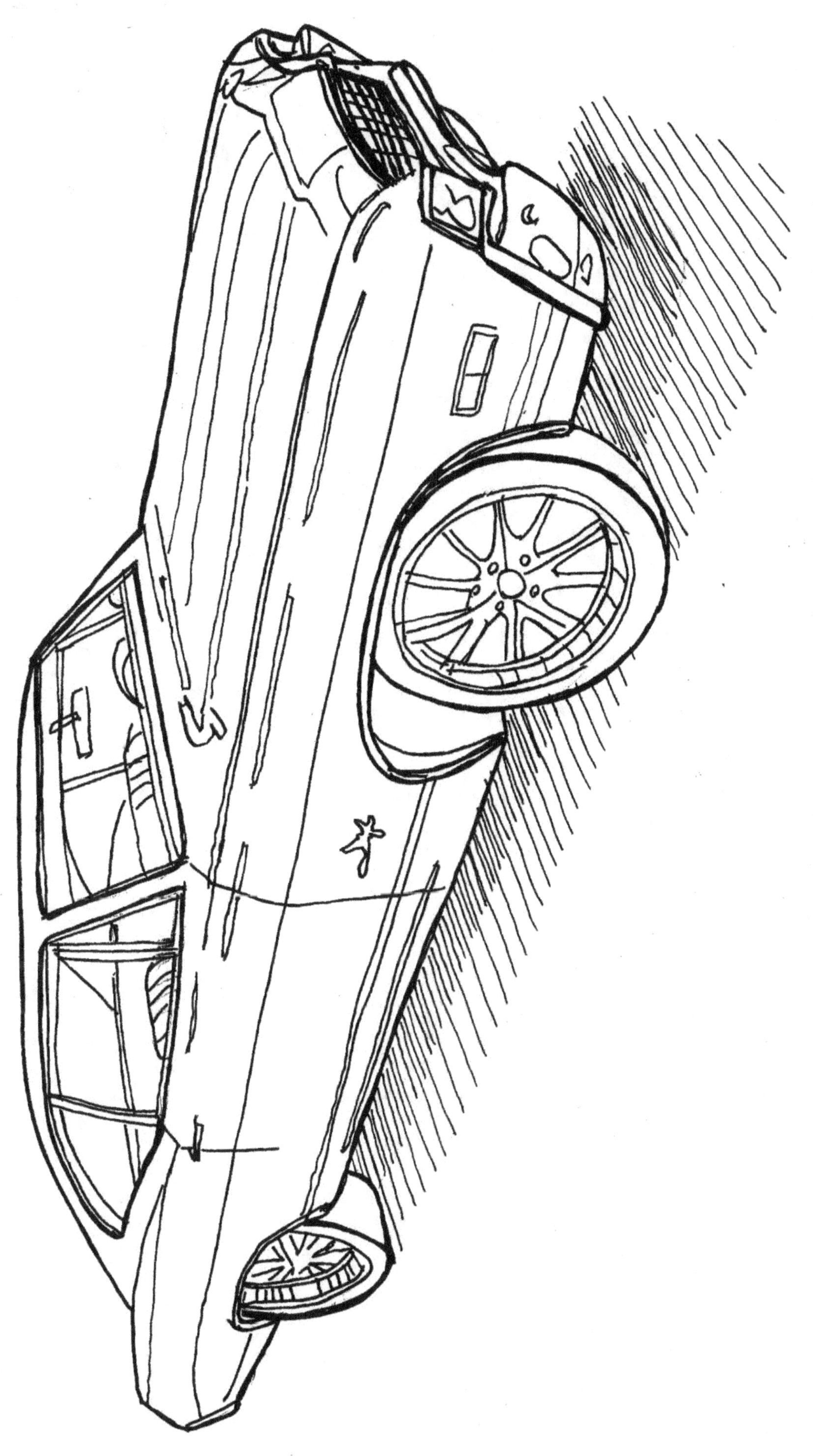

1968 CHEVROLET IMPALA

1965 CHEVROLET IMPALA

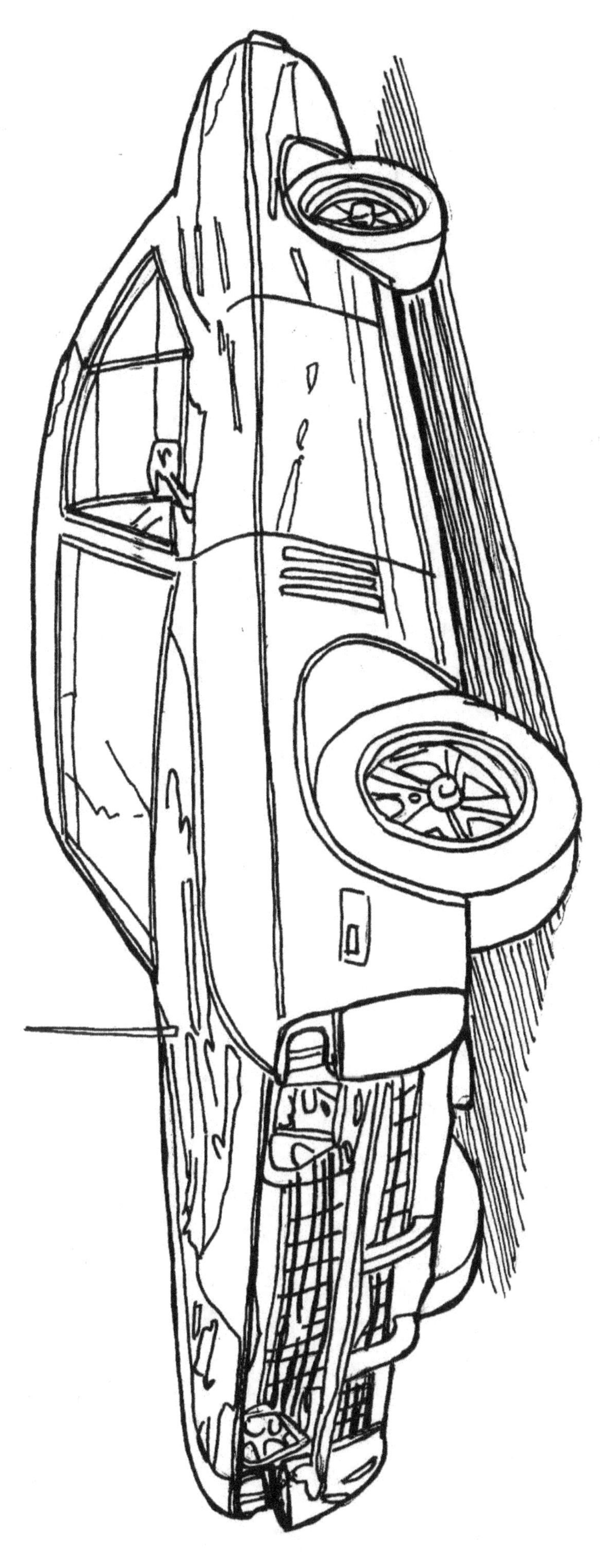

1968 CHEVROLET IMPALA

1970 PLYMOUTH GTX

1973 BUICK CENTURY

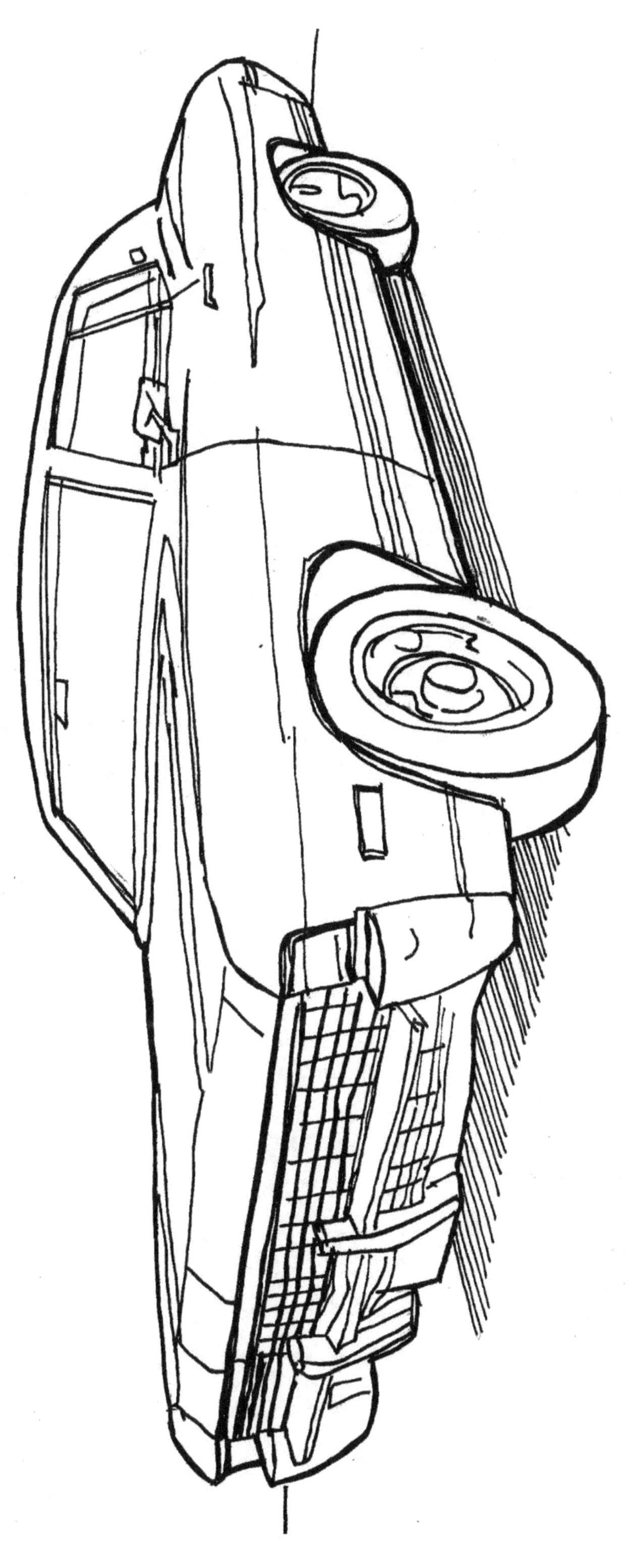

1968 CHEVROLET CAPRICE

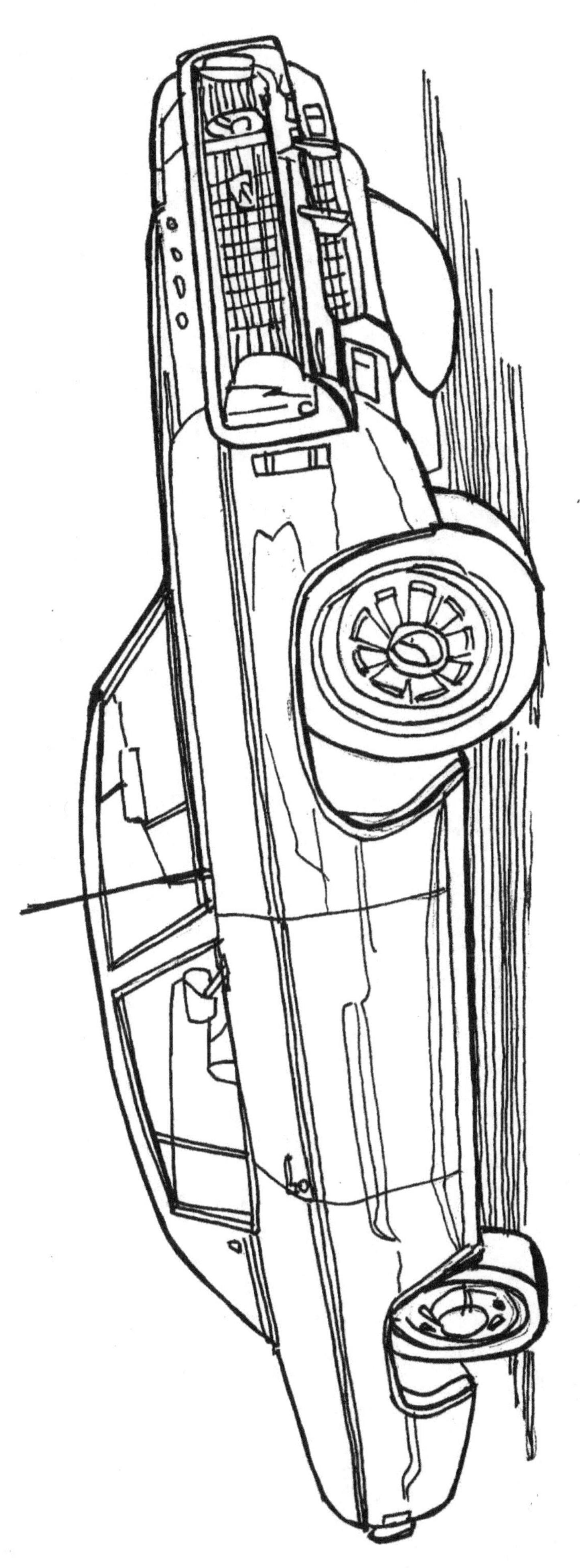

1969 CHEVROLET CAPRICE

1968 DODGE CHARGER

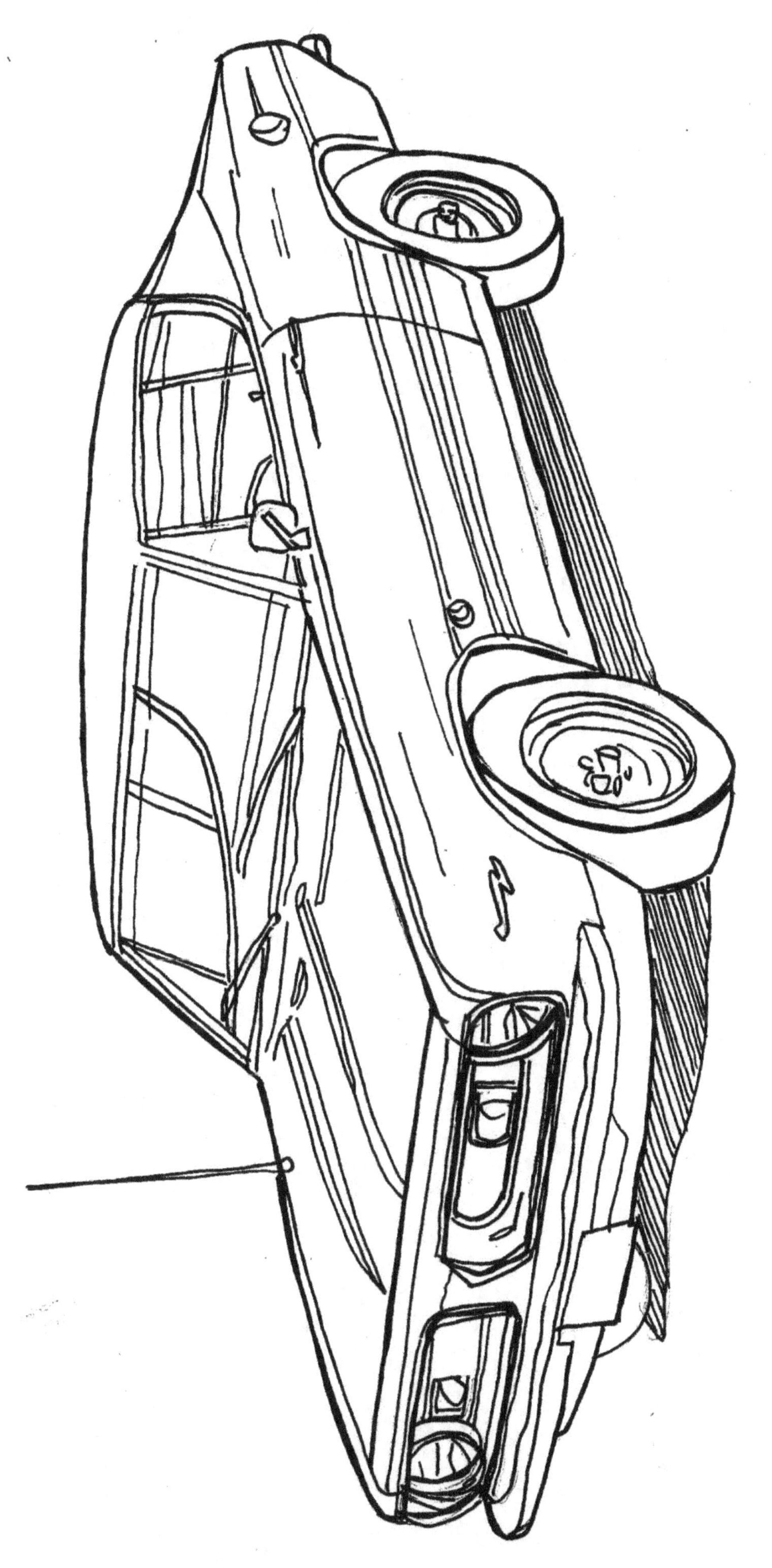

1967 PLYMOUTH BARRACUDA

1970 DODGE CHALLENGER

1969 FORD MUSTANG MARCH 1

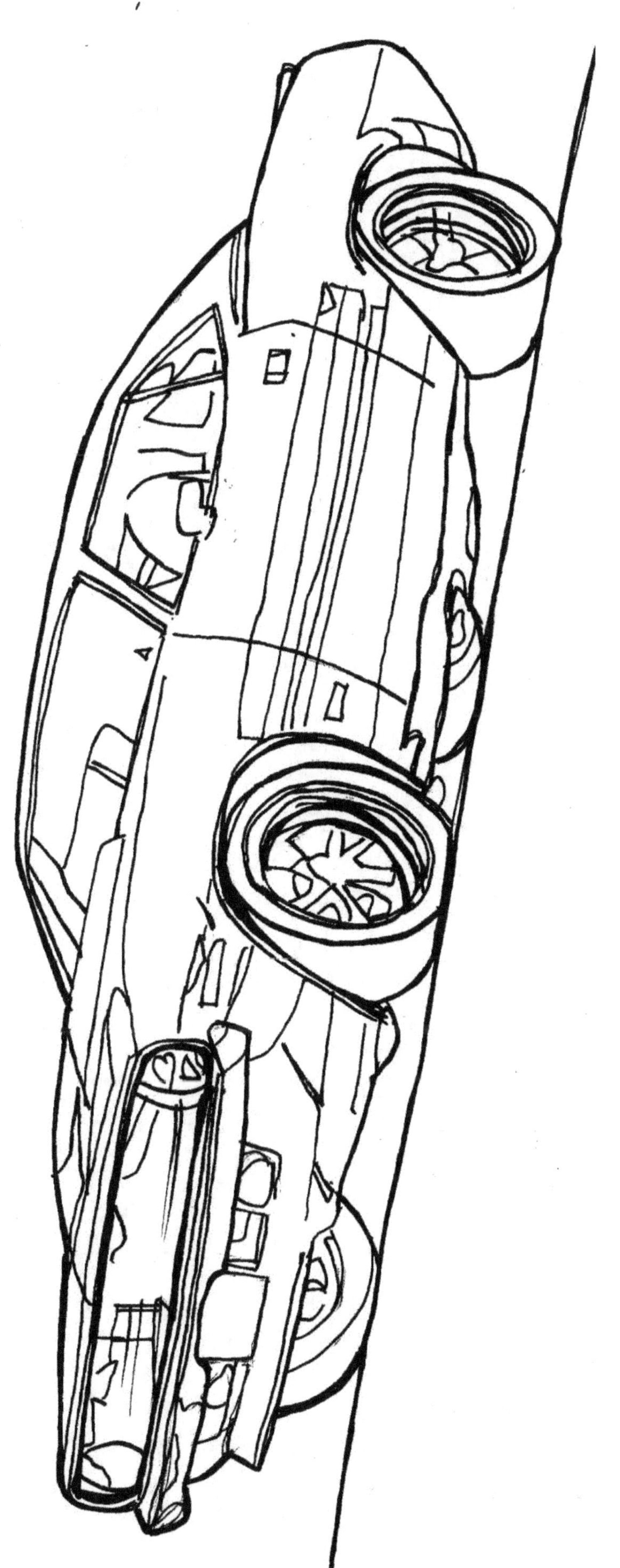

1970 PLYMOUTH BARRACUDA

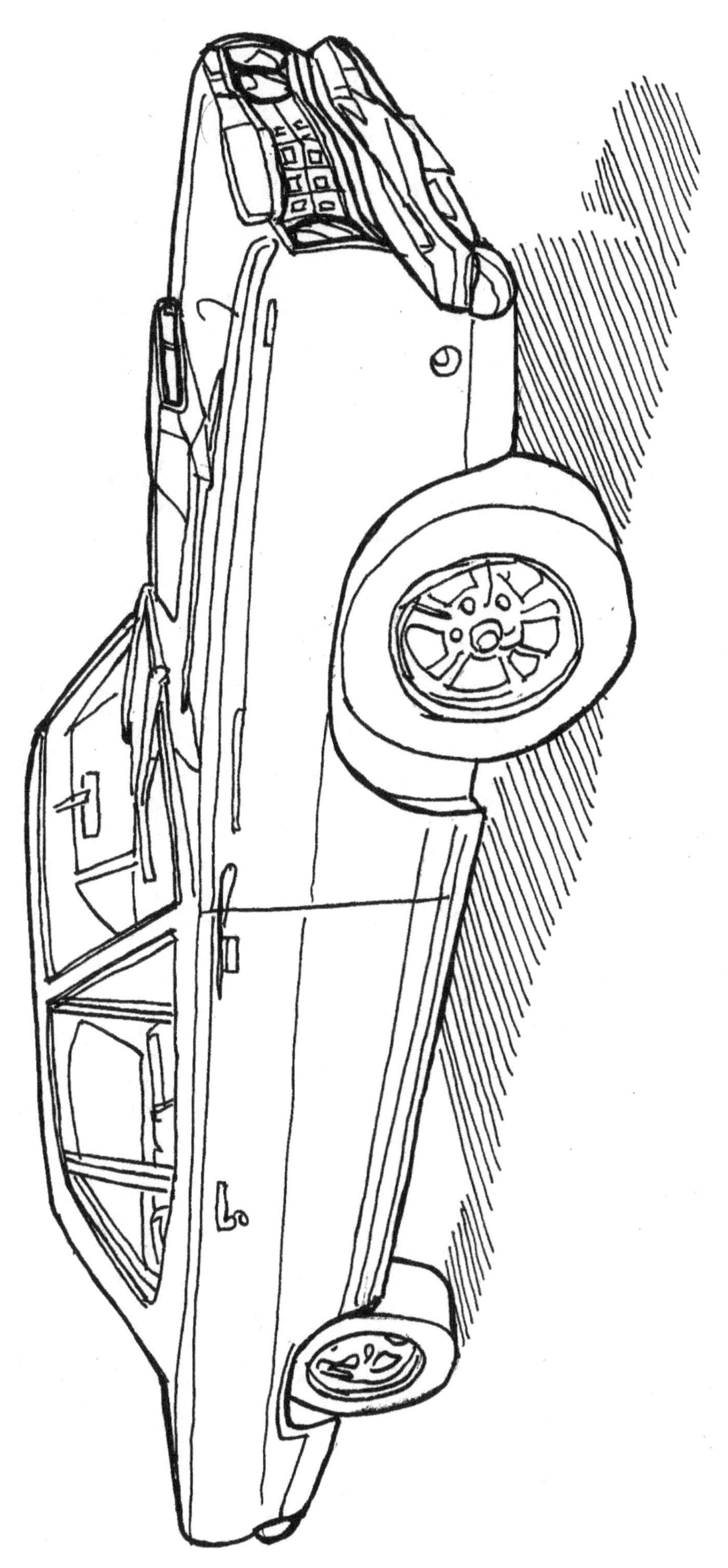

1968 PLYMOUTH ROAD RUNNER

1969 PLYMOUTH ROAD RUNNER

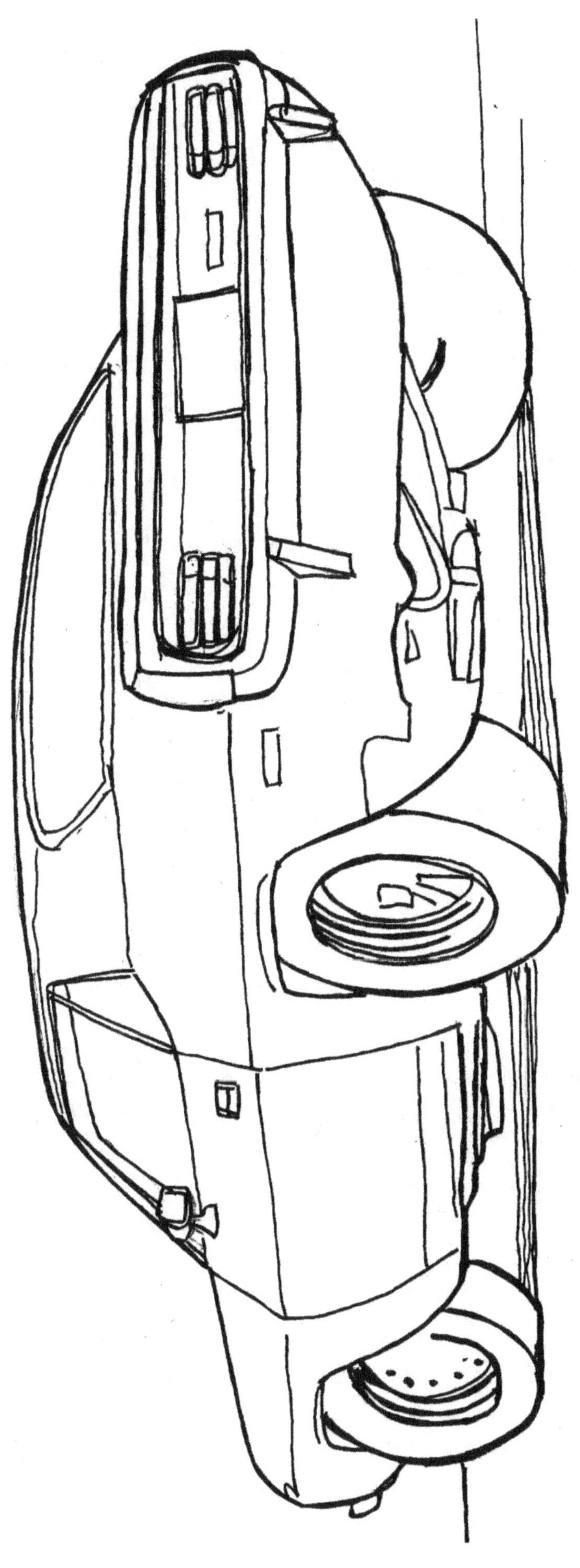

1970 PLYMOUTH BARRACUDA

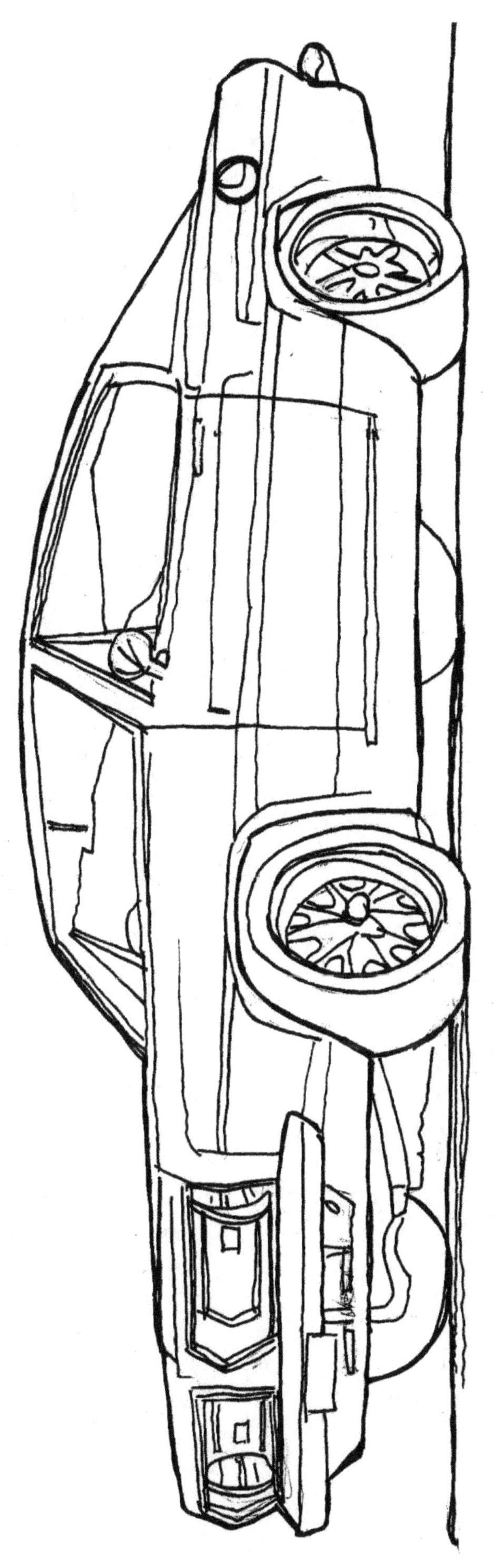

1967 PLYMOUTH BARRACUDA

1967 CHEVROLET CHEVELLE

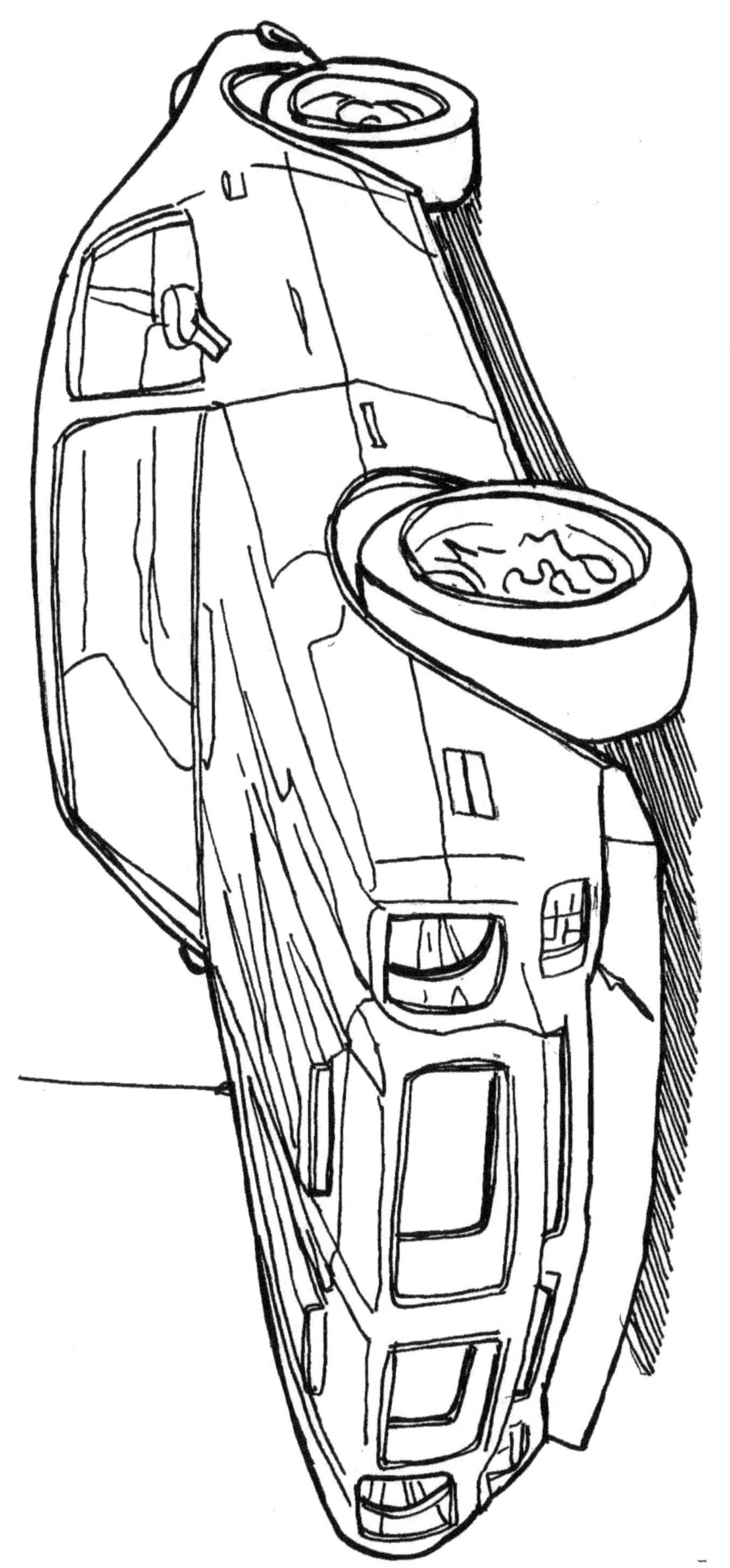

1972 PONTIAC FIREBIRD

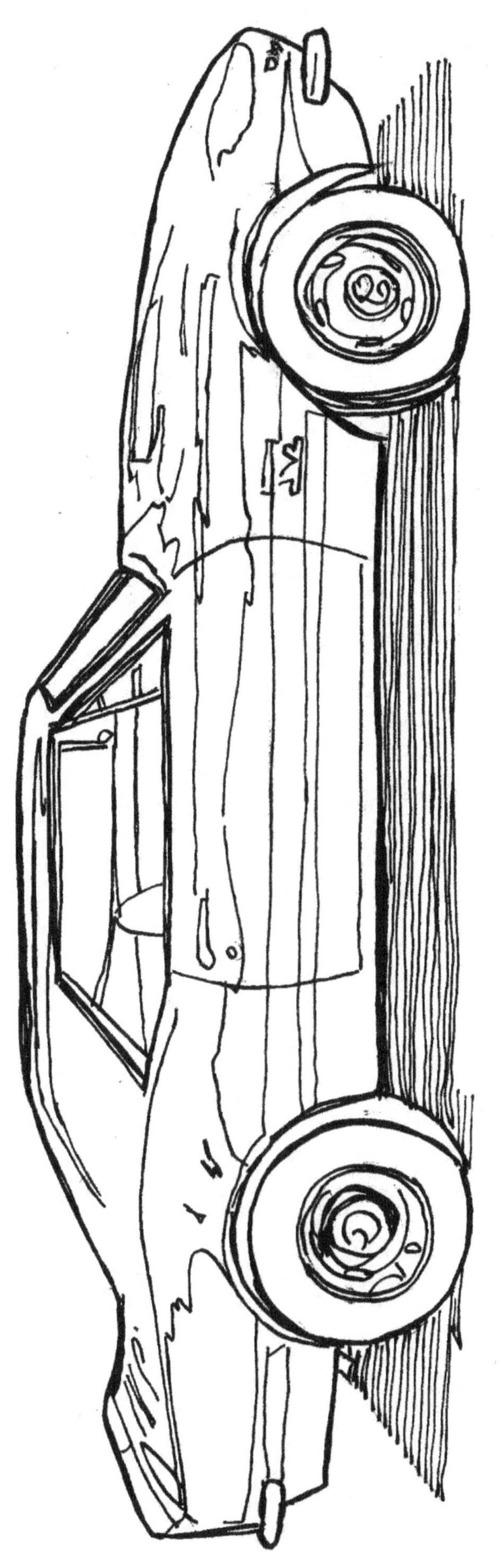

1967 CHEVROLET CAMARO

1969 PLYMOUTH ROAD RUNNER

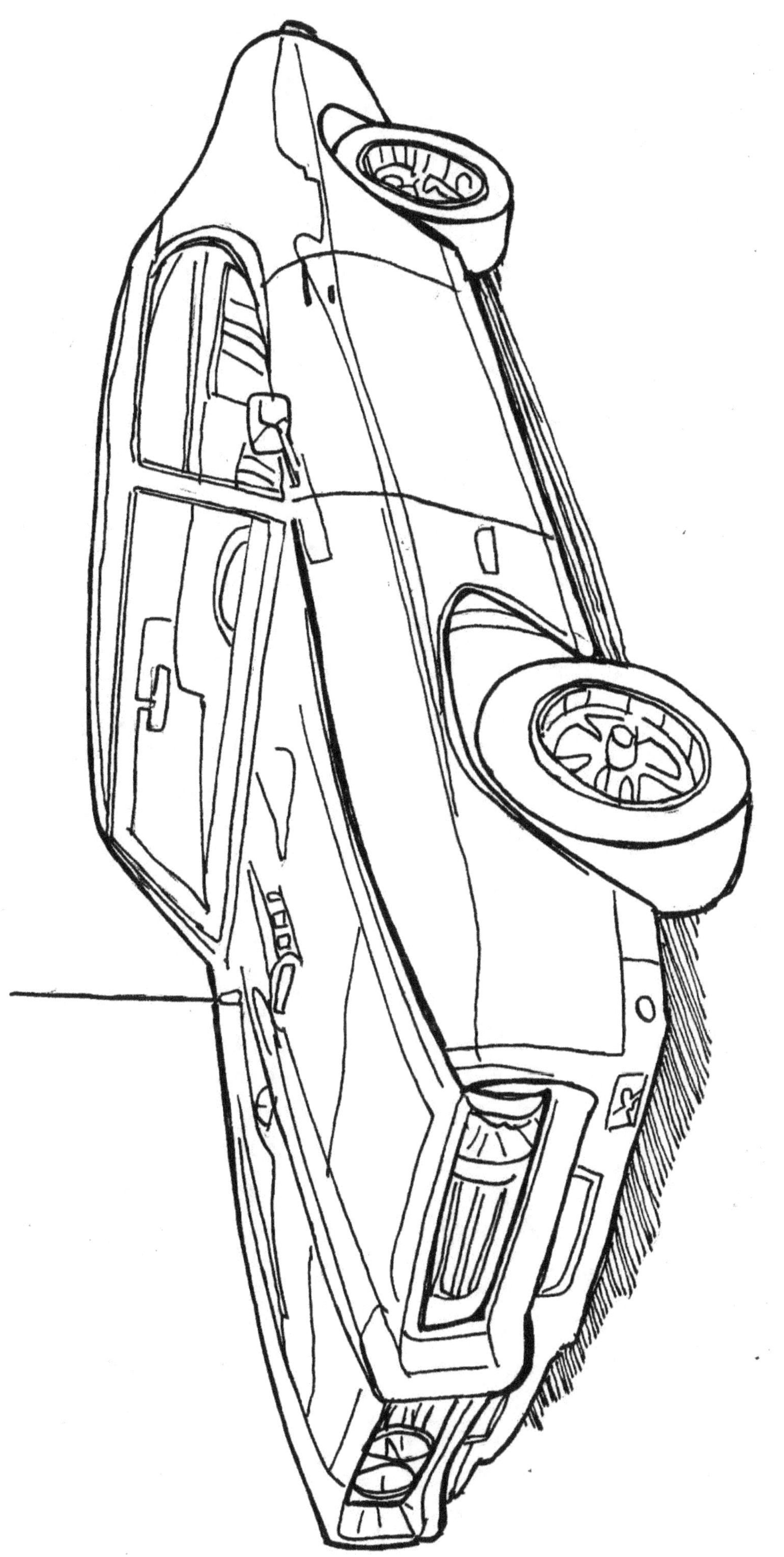

1968 PONTIAC GTO

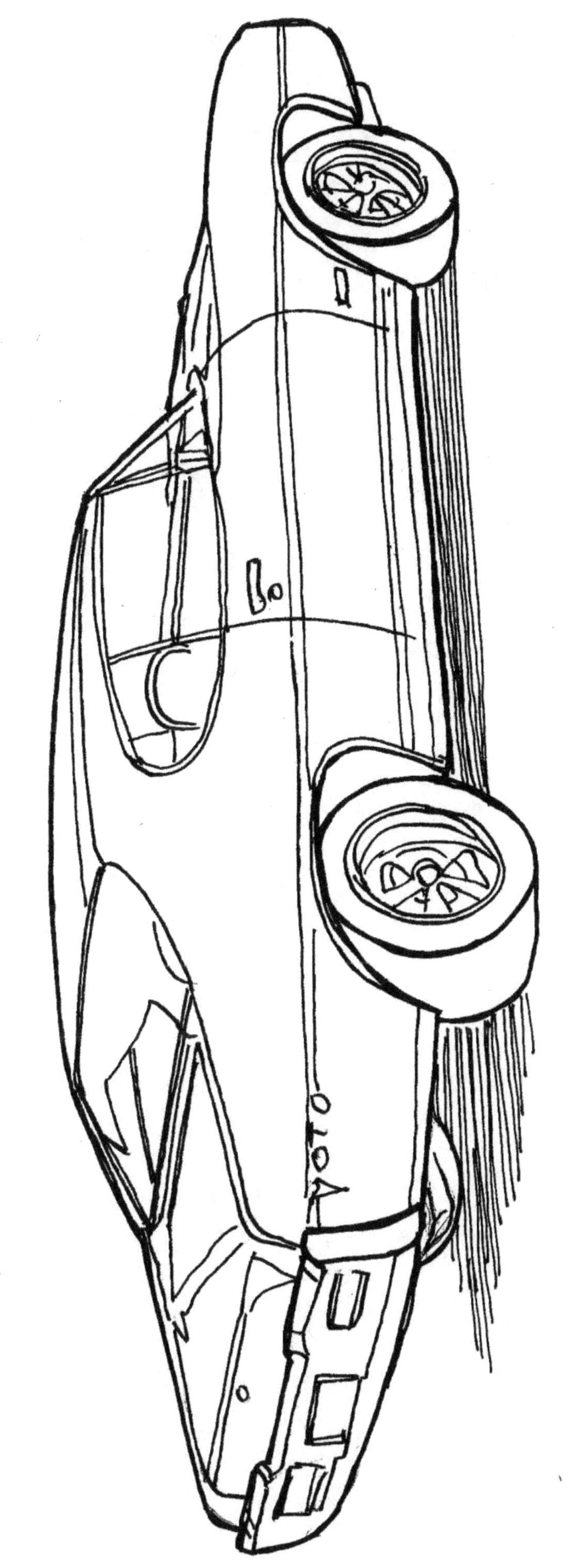

1971 PONTIAC GTO 400

1967 CHEVROLET CAMARO

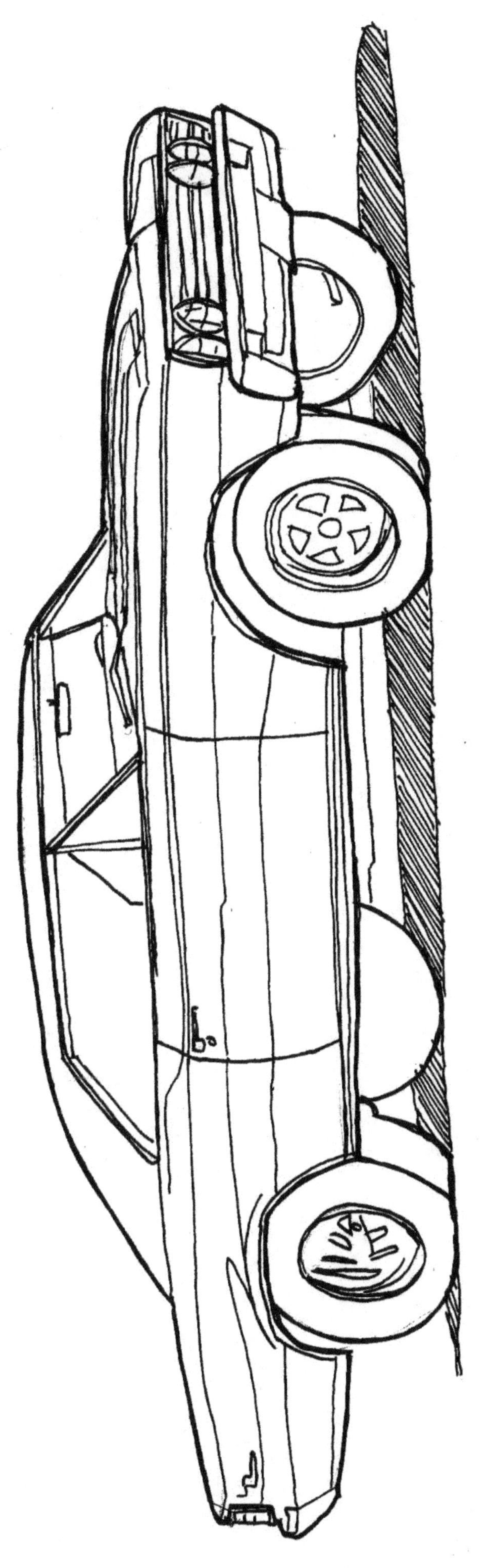
1967 CHEVROLET CHEVELLE

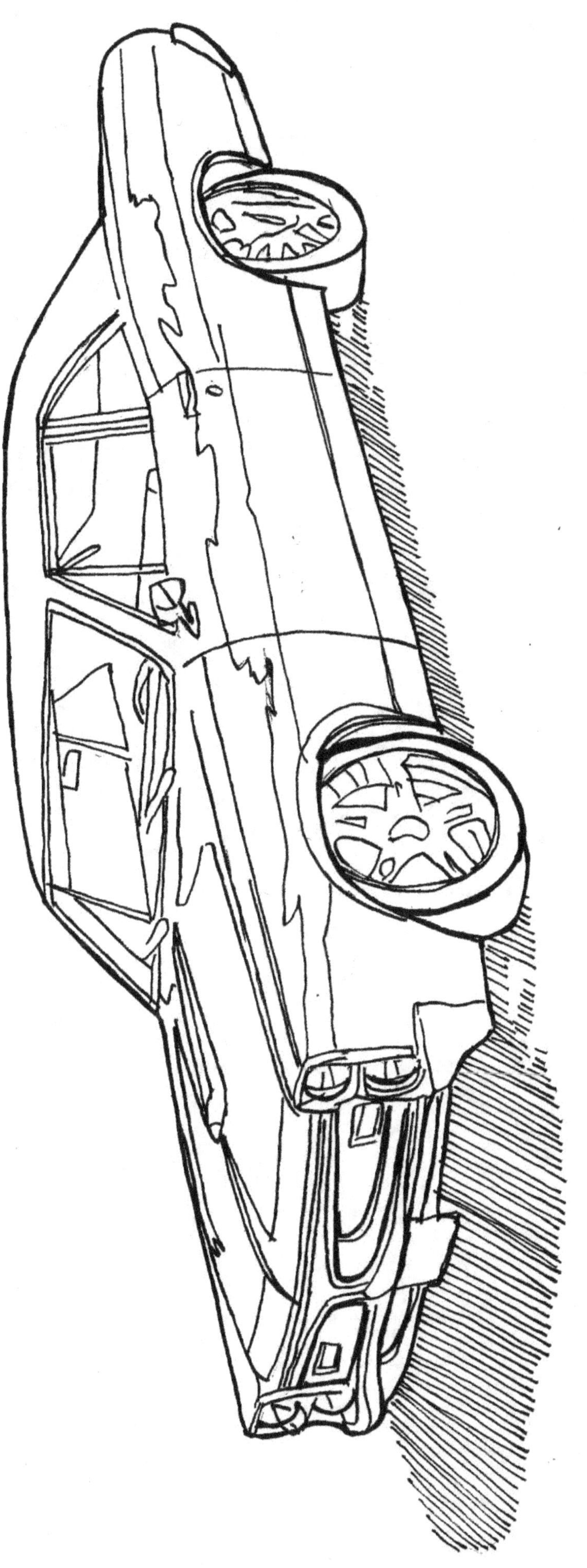

1967 PONTIAC GTO

1971 CHEVROLET CHEVELLE

1971 PONTIAC FIREBIRD

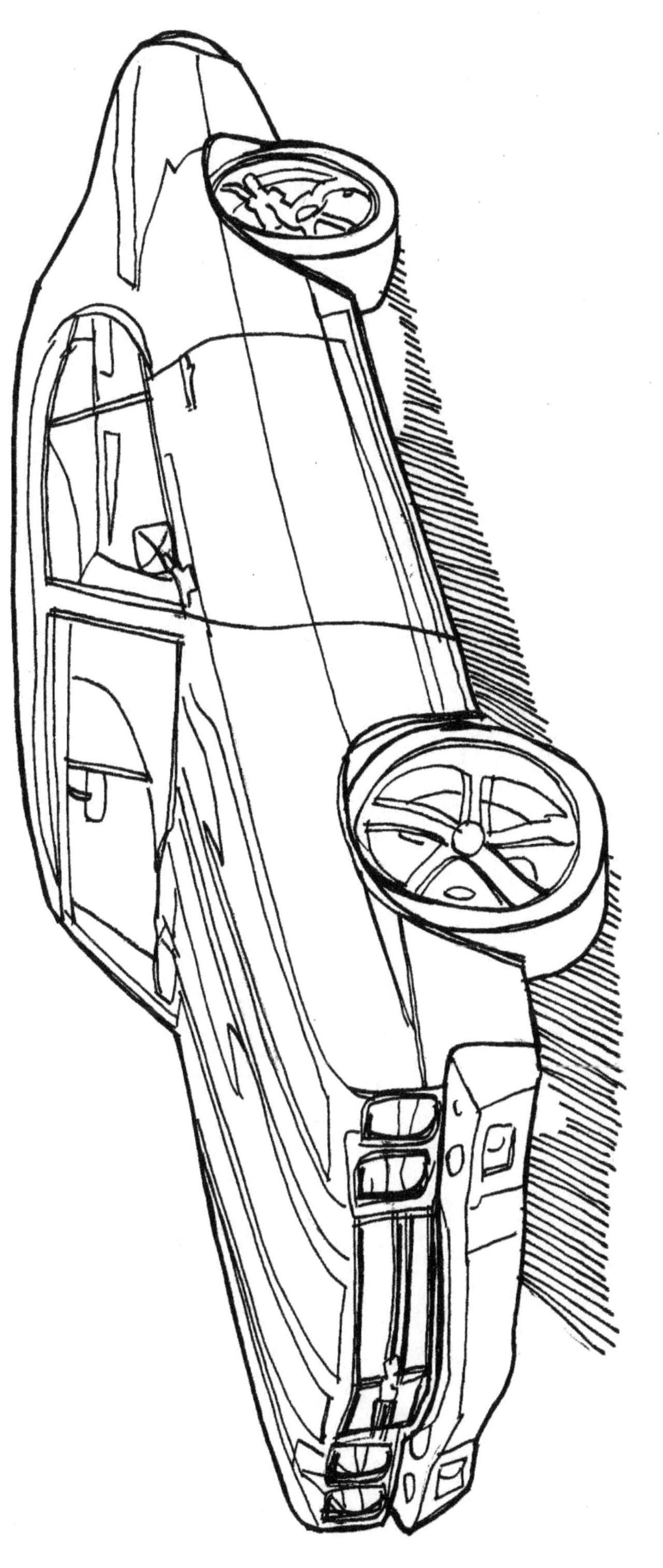

1970 CHEVROLET CHEVELLE

1972 CHEVROLET CHEVELLE

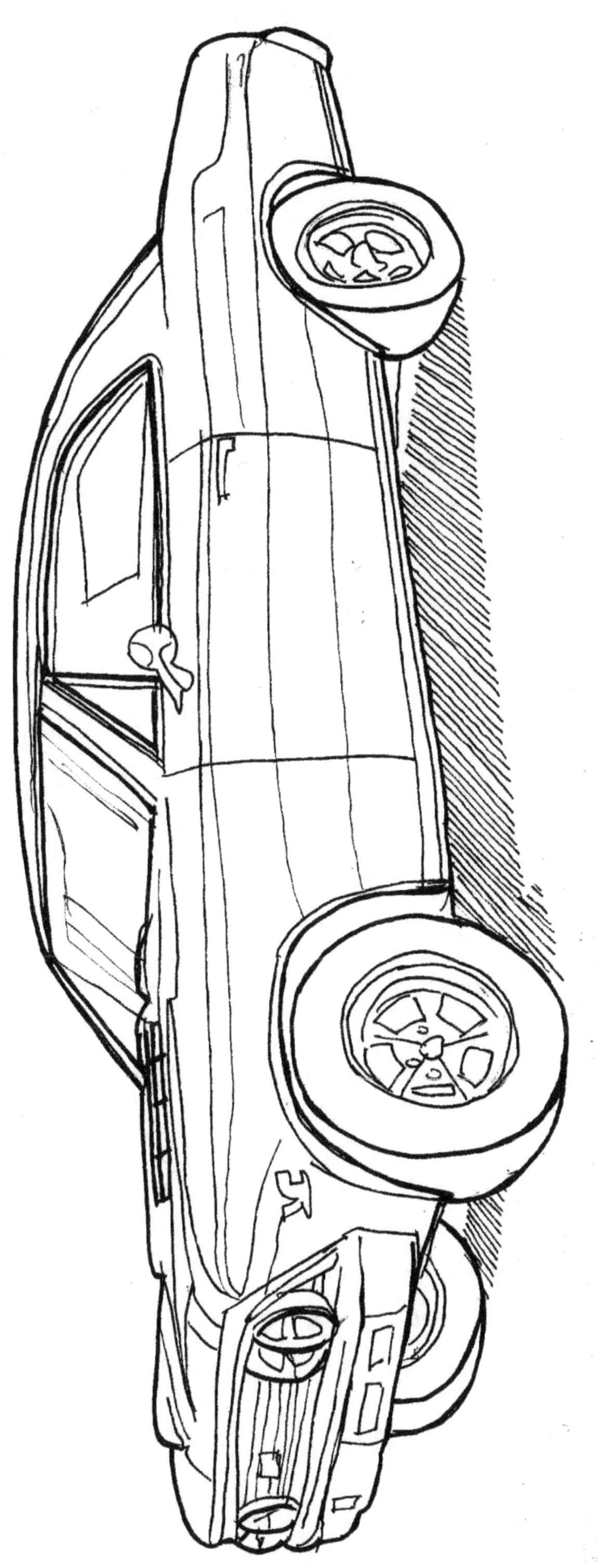

1966 CHEVROLET CHEVELLE

the same car images printed in a smaller size.
Test colors and techniques.

1970 CHEVROLET CHEVELLE

1970 DODGE CHARGER RT

1969 SHELBY MUSTANG GT350

1969 SHELBY GT500 FASTBACK

1970 FORD MUSTANG BOSS 302

1970 CORONET R/T

1969 FORD MUSTANG BOSS

1969 PONTIAC GTO

1970 CORONET SUPER BEE

1969 PONTIAC GTO

1968 CHEVROLET IMPALA

1965 CHEVROLET IMPALA

1968 CHEVROLET IMPALA

1970 PLYMOUTH GTX

1973 BUICK CENTURY

1968 CHEVROLET CAPRICE

1969 CHEVROLET CAPRICE

1968 DODGE CHARGER

1967 PLYMOUTH BARRACUDA

1970 DODGE CHALLENGER

1969 FORD MUSTANG MARCH 1

1970 PLYMOUTH BARRACUDA

1968 PLYMOUTH ROAD RUNNER

1969 PLYMOUTH ROAD RUNNER

1970 PLYMOUTH BARRACUDA

1967 PLYMOUTH BARRACUDA

1967 CHEVROLET CHEVELLE

1972 PONTIAC FIREBIRD

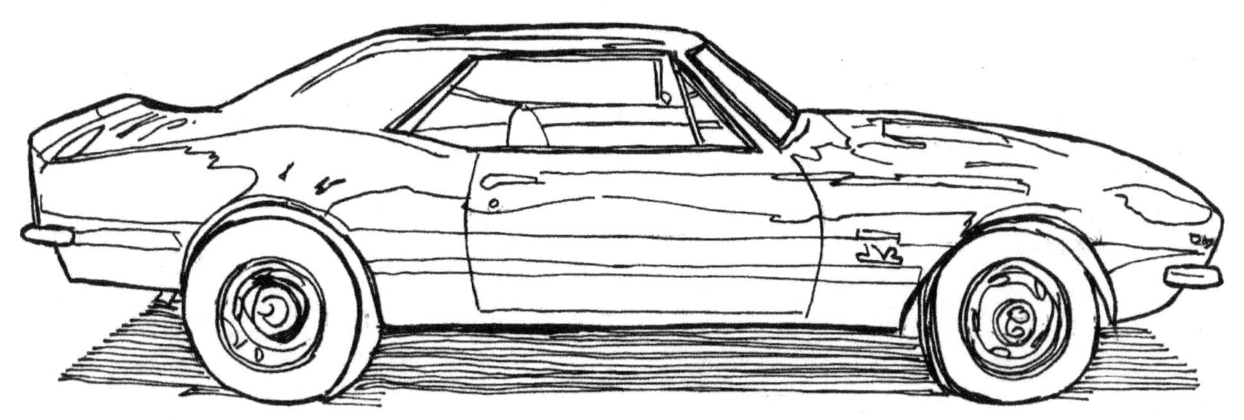

1967 CHEVROLET CAMARO

1969 PLYMOUTH ROAD RUNNER

1968 PONTIAC GTO

1971 PONTIAC GTO 400

1967 CHEVROLET CAMARO

1967 CHEVROLET CHEVELLE

1967 PONTIAC GTO

1971 CHEVROLET CHEVELLE

1971 PONTIAC FIREBIRD

1970 CHEVROLET CHEVELLE

1972 CHEVROLET CHEVELLE

1966 CHEVROLET CHEVELLE

OTHER COLORING BOOKS:

Cars

- American muscle cars coloring book for kids

- Supercars coloring book for kids

- Antique car coloring book for kids

Mandalas and patterns

- Geometric shapes and patterns coloring book

- Adult coloring book tessellations patterns

- Adult coloring book geometric patterns

- Adult coloring book circular patterns.

Quotes

- Inspirational quotes from the bible coloring book

- Money quotes coloring book

- Quotes for success coloring book

- Funny Mom Quotes and Patterns coloring book

- Motivational swear words coloring book

9 798453 412860